Our Favorite Cranberry recipes

Copyright 2020, Gooseberry Patch

Share your homemade goodies with a friend. Wrap muffins or scones in a tea towel and tuck them into a basket along with a jar of jam. A sweet gift that says "I'm thinking of you!"

White Chocolate-Cranberry Scones

Makes 8 scones

1-1/2 c. biscuit baking mix
2 T. sugar
1/2 c. fresh cranberries, chopped,
  or sweetened dried cranberries
1/2 to 3/4 c. white chocolate chips

Optional: 1 t. orange zest
1 egg, beaten
3 to 4 T. milk
Optional: powdered sugar

In a large bowl, gently toss together baking mix, sugar and cranberries. Mix in chocolate chips and zest, if using; set aside. In a small bowl, whisk together egg and milk; add to baking mix. Use a fork to mix together gently. With a large cookie scoop, portion out 8 scoops of dough onto a parchment paper-lined baking sheet. Flatten each scone slightly, using moistened hands. Bake 400 degrees for 10 minutes, or until edges are turning golden. Drizzle Orange Glaze over cooled scones; dust with powdered sugar, if desired.

Orange Glaze:

1/2 c. powdered sugar

1 to 2 t. orange juice

Combine powdered sugar with enough orange juice to make a drizzling consistency.

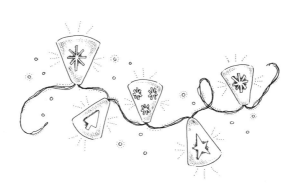

String small nutmeg graters on a set of white lights
for a sweet kitchen garland.

4

French Toast with Honey Cranberries

5 eggs, beaten
2/3 c. milk
1/4 c. sugar
1 t. vanilla extract
4 T. butter, divided

8 slices whole-grain or
white bread
4 to 6 thin slices Brie cheese
Optional: warmed honey

Make Honey Cranberries ahead of time. In a shallow dish, whisk together eggs, milk, sugar and vanilla; set aside. Melt 2 tablespoons butter in a large non-stick skillet over medium heat. Dip 2 slices of bread into egg mixture until well coated. Add to skillet and cook for 3 to 5 minutes per side, until golden. Repeat with remaining butter and bread. Arrange French toast slices on a serving plate, alternating with slices of cheese and spoonfuls of Honey Cranberries. Serve with honey on the side, if desired.

Honey Cranberries:

2 T. butter
2 c. fresh or frozen cranberries

1/3 c. honey

Melt butter in a saucepan over medium heat; add cranberries and honey. Cook until cranberries are soft and honey has thickened, about 3 minutes.

Doughnut hole kabobs...what a delicious idea!
Slide bite-size doughnut holes onto wooden skewers
and stand the skewers in a tall vase for easy serving.

Rocky Mountain Cereal Bars   *Makes about 2-1/2 dozen*

2/3 c. sugar
2/3 c. corn syrup
1 c. creamy peanut butter
6 c. doughnut-shaped multi-grain
    oat cereal

3/4 to 1 c. sweetened dried
    cranberries

Combine sugar, corn syrup and peanut butter in a large saucepan over low heat. Cook, stirring constantly, until peanut butter is melted. Remove from heat. Add cereal and cranberries; mix well. Spread cereal mixture evenly into a lightly greased 13"x9" baking pan. Cool completely; cut into bars.

Fresh fruit salad is a scrumptious, healthy side that
just about everyone will love. Slice up oranges, strawberries
and kiwi fruit and toss with a simple dressing made of
equal parts honey and lemon or orange juice.

Nanny's Cranberry Biscuit Ring

Serves 5 to 6

1/3 c. butter, melted
1/4 c. honey
1/2 c. whole-berry cranberry sauce

2 7-1/2 oz. tubes refrigerated
  biscuits

Spread melted butter in the bottom of a Bundt® pan; add honey and cranberry sauce. Stand biscuits on their side around pan, forming a ring. Bake at 350 degrees for 12 to 15 minutes, until biscuits are set and lightly golden. Cover pan with a plate; turn biscuits out onto plate. Spoon out any remaining topping; spread evenly over biscuits.

Make fancy bacon curls to garnish breakfast plates. Fry bacon until
browned but not crisp, immediately roll up slices and
fasten each with a toothpick. Drain on paper towels. Mmm!

Sausage-Cranberry Quiche

Makes 6 servings

1/2 lb. sage-flavored ground
   pork sausage
1/4 c. onion, chopped
3/4 c. sweetened dried cranberries
9-inch pie crust, unbaked

1-1/2 c. shredded Monterey
   Jack cheese
3 eggs, beaten
1-1/2 c. half-and-half

In a large skillet over medium-high heat, brown sausage with onion;
drain. Remove from heat and stir in cranberries. Line a 9" pie plate with
pie crust. Sprinkle cheese into pie crust; evenly spoon in sausage mixture.
In a bowl, combine eggs and half-and-half; whisk until mixed but not
frothy. Pour egg mixture over sausage mixture. Bake at 375 degrees for
40 to 45 minutes, until a knife tip inserted in the center comes out clean.
Let stand for 10 minutes; cut into wedges.

Planning a midday brunch? Along with breakfast foods like baked eggs, coffee cake and cereal, offer a light, savory main dish or two for those who have already enjoyed breakfast.

Cranberry-Pecan Coffee Cake

Makes 6 to 8 servings

1 c. sweetened dried cranberries
1 c. boiling water
1-1/2 c. butter, melted
2/3 c. sugar
2 eggs, beaten

1 t. vanilla extract
1-1/2 c. all-purpose flour
1/2 c. toasted chopped pecans
Garnish: powdered sugar

Cover cranberries with hot water; let stand for 10 minutes and drain. In a bowl, combine melted butter and sugar; stir in eggs and vanilla. Add flour and pecans; fold in cranberries. Pour batter into a buttered 8" round springform or torte pan. Bake at 350 degrees for 45 minutes. Cool; dust with powdered sugar. Cut into wedges to serve.

Watch for old-fashioned cream pitchers at tag sales...
set out a variety of sweet toppings like flavored syrups
and honey for fluffy pancakes and waffles.

Whipping Cream Waffles & Cranberry Butter

Makes 2 servings

8-oz. container whipping cream
2 eggs, separated
1 T. butter, melted and
    slightly cooled

2/3 c. all-purpose flour
1/3 c. sugar
1 t. baking powder
1/8 t. salt

In a deep bowl, beat cream with an electric mixer on medium speed until soft peaks form. In a separate bowl, beat egg yolks with a fork until thick and light-colored; fold in whipped cream and butter. Combine remaining ingredients in a small bowl; fold into whipped cream mixture. Beat egg whites on high speed until stiff peaks form; fold into batter. Batter will be thick. For each waffle, spoon half of batter onto a preheated, oiled waffle iron, spreading to edges. Bake according to manufacturer's directions, until crisp and lightly golden. Serve with Cranberry Butter.

Cranberry Butter:

1/2 c. butter, softened
1/4 c. powdered sugar

2 T. whole-berry cranberry sauce

Combine butter and powdered sugar; beat with an electric mixer on medium speed until blended. Stir in cranberry sauce; chill.

Always turn your slow cooker off, unplug it from
the electrical outlet and allow it to cool before cleaning.
The outside of the heating base may be cleaned
with a soft cloth and warm soapy water.

Special-Morning Oatmeal

Serves 4

1/3 c. brown sugar, packed
2 t. cinnamon
1 t. nutmeg
2 apples, peeled, cored and
    thinly sliced
3/4 c. sweetened dried cranberries

1/4 c. butter, sliced
2 c. old-fashioned oats, uncooked
2 c. water
1 c. apple juice
1 c. cranberry juice cocktail

In a bowl, mix brown sugar, cinnamon and nutmeg. Add apples and cranberries; toss to coat. Transfer to a slow cooker; dot with butter. Combine oats, water and juices; spoon over fruit mixture in slow cooker. Do not stir. Cover and cook on low setting for 7 to 8 hours. Stir before serving.

A loaf of homemade fruit bread is always a welcome gift.
Make sure it stays fresh and tasty...let the bread cool
completely, then wrap well in plastic wrap or aluminum foil.

Mom's Christmas Morning Cranberry Bread

Makes one loaf

2 c. all-purpose flour
1 c. sugar
1-1/2 t. baking powder
1/4 t. baking soda
1/2 t. salt
1/3 c. butter

1 egg, lightly beaten
1 t. orange zest
2/3 c. orange juice
1-1/2 c. fresh cranberries, halved
1 c. nuts, coarsely chopped

In a large bowl, stir together flour, sugar, baking powder, baking soda and salt. Cut in butter with a fork until mixture looks like coarse crumbs; set aside. In a small bowl, whisk together egg, orange zest and juice. Add to flour mixture and stir until moistened. Fold in cranberries and nuts. Spoon batter into a lightly greased 9"x5" loaf pan. Bake at 350 degrees for 60 to 70 minutes, until a toothpick inserted in center tests done. Cool loaf in pan on a wire rack for about 10 minutes. Remove from pan; cool completely. Wrap and store overnight before slicing.

A baker's secret! Grease muffin cups on the bottoms
and just halfway up the sides...the muffins will
bake up nicely puffed on top.

Cranberry Upside-Down Muffins *Makes 1-1/2 dozen*

2-1/2 c. all-purpose flour
1/2 c. sugar
1 T. baking powder
1/2 t. salt

1-1/4 c. milk
1/3 c. butter, melted
1 egg, beaten

Combine flour, sugar, baking powder and salt in a large bowl; mix well. Add milk, butter and egg; stir just until moistened and set aside. Prepare Cranberry Topping; spoon topping into 18 greased muffin cups. Spoon batter over topping, filling each cup 2/3 full. Bake at 400 degrees for 20 to 25 minutes, until a toothpick tests clean. Immediately invert onto a wire rack set over wax paper; serve warm. Makes 1-1/2 dozen.

Cranberry Topping:

1/3 c. brown sugar, packed
1/4 c. butter
1/2 t. cinnamon

1/2 c. fresh cranberries, halved
1/2 c. chopped nuts

Combine ingredients in a small saucepan. Cook over medium heat until brown sugar is dissolved.

A touch of whimsy...use Grandma's old cow-shaped
pitcher to serve milk or cream for breakfast
cereal, oatmeal and coffee.

Cranberry-Carrot Loaf

Makes one loaf

2 c. all-purpose flour
3/4 c. sugar
1-1/2 t. baking powder
1-1/2 t. baking soda
1/4 t. salt
1/2 t. cinnamon

1/2 c. carrot, peeled and shredded
1/3 c. light sour cream
1/4 c. unsweetened applesauce
1/4 c. water
2 eggs, lightly beaten
1 c. frozen cranberries

Grease the bottom of a 9"x5" loaf pan; set aside. In a large bowl, mix together flour, sugar, baking powder, baking soda, salt and cinnamon. Stir in carrot to coat. Make a well in center of flour mixture; add sour cream, applesauce, water and eggs. Stir until combined. Slowly stir in cranberries. Spoon batter into pan. Bake on center oven rack at 350 degrees for 60 minutes, or until a toothpick inserted in the center comes out clean. Cool loaf in pan for 15 minutes. Remove to a rack and cool completely.

Add a splash of color to sparkling cider and lemonade.
Freeze grape or cranberry juice in ice cube trays and
add a few to drinking glasses...so pretty!

Patriotic Bread

Makes one loaf

3 c. all-purpose flour
1 t. baking powder
1 t. baking soda
1 t. salt
1 c. sugar

1/2 c. butter, softened
2 eggs, beaten
1 c. buttermilk
1 c. whole-berry cranberry sauce
1 c. blueberries

Combine flour, baking powder, baking soda and salt; set aside. Blend sugar and butter together in a large bowl; blend in eggs and buttermilk. Add flour mixture; mix well. Stir in cranberry sauce and blueberries; pour into a greased 9"x5" loaf pan. Bake at 375 degrees for one hour and 10 minutes, or until a toothpick inserted in the center comes out clean. Remove loaf from pan; cool on a wire rack.

When you rise in the morning, form a resolution to make
the day a happy one for a fellow creature.

—Sydney Smith

Beckie's Cranberry Bran Muffins   *Makes 16 muffins*

2 c. bran & raisin cereal
1/2 c. very hot water
1 c. self-rising flour
1 t. baking powder
1/2 c. sugar
3 T. powdered sweetener
1 t. cinnamon

1/4 t. allspice
1/2 c. canola oil
2 eggs, beaten
1/4 c. walnuts, diced
1/4 c. sweetened dried cranberries
1/4 c. ground flax seed

Add cereal to a 2-cup glass measuring cup; add hot water. Set aside; do not stir. In a bowl, combine flour, baking powder, sugar, sweetener and spices; stir well. Add remaining ingredients; stir well. Fold in cereal mixture; batter will be thick. Spoon batter into 16 greased muffin cups, filling 3/4 full. Bake at 375 degrees for 12 to 15 minutes.

Snowy paper-white narcissus flowers are a winter delight
that Grandmother loved. Place paper-white bulbs in
water-filled bulb vases, pointed ends up. Set in a sunny
window. In about 6 weeks you'll have blooms!

Cranberry Yeast Rolls

Makes 2 dozen

2 envs. active dry yeast
1/4 c. very warm water,
    110 to 115 degrees
1 c. very warm milk, 110 to
    115 degrees
1/2 c. butter, sliced
1/4 c. sugar

1 t. salt
4 c. all-purpose flour, divided
2 eggs, beaten
15-oz. can whole-berry cranberry
    sauce
1 t. cinnamon, divided

In a cup, dissolve yeast in warm water; set aside. In a large bowl, pour warm milk over butter, sugar and salt. Let stand for 5 to 10 minutes. Add yeast mixture to milk mixture. Stir in 2 cups flour; beat in eggs. Add remaining flour and mix well. Cover and refrigerate dough for 2 hours to overnight. Divide dough in half. Roll out half of dough on a floured surface to 1/4-inch thick. Spread half of cranberry sauce over dough, to 1/4-inch from edge of dough. Sprinkle with 1/2 teaspoon cinnamon. Roll up dough, starting on one long edge; slice into 12 spirals. Place rolls cut-side down in a greased 13"x9" baking pan. Repeat with remaining dough, sauce, cinnamon and another pan. Cover pans and let rise for 30 minutes. Bake at 350 degrees for 25 to 30 minutes, until golden.

Go out to greet the sunrise! Wrap warm breakfast
breads or muffins in a vintage tea towel before tucking
into a basket...add a thermos of hot coffee or spiced tea.

Pretty Pecan-Cranberry Butter *Makes about 1-1/3 cups*

3/4 c. butter, softened
2 T. brown sugar, packed
2 T. light corn syrup

1 c. fresh cranberries, chopped
2 T. chopped pecans, toasted

In a small bowl, using a whisk or an electric mixer on low speed, beat butter, brown sugar and corn syrup until fluffy, about 5 minutes. Add cranberries and pecans; beat 5 minutes longer, or until butter turns pink. Transfer mixture to a sheet of plastic wrap; shape into a log. Wrap; chill.

Keep fruit punch from becoming diluted, with an ice ring made of juice! Just freeze cranberry or pineapple juice in an angel food cake pan and pop it out.

Jubilee Bubbly Punch

2 15-oz. cans jellied cranberry
   sauce
1-1/2 c. orange juice

1/2 c. lemon juice
2 1-ltr. bottles ginger ale, chilled

In a large pitcher or punch bowl, whisk cranberry sauce until smooth. Stir in orange juice and lemon juice. Chill until serving time. Just before serving, add ginger ale.

Warming beverages are a must at any autumn get-together!
Whip up some name tags to slip onto mug handles. Stamp or write
names on metal-rimmed round paper tags. Slide onto precut
loops of memory wire along with a decorative charm.
A craft store will have all the supplies you need.

Cranberry-Orange Warmer

16-oz. pkg. frozen cranberries,
    thawed
4-inch cinnamon stick
8 c. water
6-oz. can frozen orange juice
    concentrate, thawed

6-oz. can frozen lemonade
    concentrate, thawed
1 c. sugar

In a saucepan, bring cranberries, cinnamon stick and water to a boil. Boil for 5 minutes. Strain, discarding cranberries and cinnamon stick. Return juice to saucepan. Add juice concentrates and sugar to saucepan; stir until sugar melts. Serve warm.

Paper cupcake liners come in all colors...great for
serving single portions of chips or party mix!

Pink Lassies

1 c. cranberry juice cocktail   1 c. vanilla ice cream
1/4 c. orange juice

Combine all ingredients in a blender. Cover and blend until smooth. Serve in tall glasses with straws.

A fun icebreaker for a large gathering of all ages! Divide into
two teams...the goal is to line up alphabetically by everyone's
first names. After 60 seconds, blow a whistle
and have each team sound off by name. The team with
the most participants in alphabetical order wins!

Hot Cranberry Punch

Makes 12 to 14 servings

64-oz. bottle cranberry juice
cocktail
12-oz. can frozen orange juice
concentrate
12-oz. can frozen pineapple
juice concentrate

3 c. water
1 t. cinnamon
Garnish: orange slices, cinnamon
sticks

In a 5-quart saucepan, combine cranberry juice, frozen juice concentrates, water and cinnamon. Simmer over medium-low heat, stirring occasionally, until frozen juice melts and is well blended. At serving time, carefully float orange slices and cinnamon sticks on top of punch.

From autumn through Christmas, a mug of spiced cider will
warm you through & through. If you enjoy making it often,
save time by filling small muslin bags ahead of time with
the whole spices, then just toss into a pot of cider as needed.

Sally's Spiced Cider

Makes 10 to 12 servings

8 c. apple juice
3 c. cranberry juice cocktail
1 t. whole cloves

1 t. whole allspice
6 4-inch cinnamon sticks
1 orange, quartered

Combine fruit juices in a 4-quart slow cooker. Place cloves and allspice in a tea ball. Add to juice mixture along with cinnamon sticks and orange wedges. Cover and cook on high setting for 30 minutes, or until heated through. Discard spices before serving.

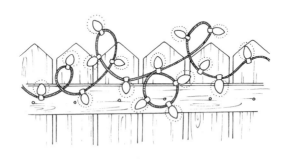

Partying outdoors? Wind sparkling white lights along
the garden fence and in the trees for a twinkling
firefly effect as the sun sets.

Cranberry Chicken Salad Bites

Makes 2 dozen

24 frozen mini pastry shells
4 c. cooked chicken, finely
   chopped
3 stalks celery, diced
1 c. sweetened dried cranberries

1/3 c. chopped pecans
1-1/2 c. mayonnaise
1/3 c. honey, or more to taste
1/4 t. salt
1/4 t. pepper

Bake pastry shells according to package directions; let cool. Meanwhile, in a large bowl, combine chicken, celery, cranberries and pecans. Mix remaining ingredients in a separate bowl; add to chicken mixture and stir gently until combined. Spoon into pastry shells and serve.

This is my invariable advice to people:
Learn how to cook...try new recipes,
learn from your mistakes, be fearless,
and above all, have fun!

—Julia Child

Bruschetta with Cranberry Relish

Serves 16

1 large whole-grain baguette loaf,
    sliced 1/4-inch thick
1 to 2 T. olive oil
1 t. orange zest
1 t. lemon zest
1/2 c. chopped pecans
1/2 c. crumbled blue cheese

Brush baguette slices lightly with oil. Arrange on a sheet pan; toast lightly under broiler. Turn slices over; spread with Cranberry Relish. Sprinkle with zests, pecans and blue cheese. Place under broiler just until cheese begins to melt.

Cranberry Relish:

16-oz. can whole-berry cranberry
    sauce
6-oz. pkg. sweetened dried
    cranberries
1/2 c. sugar
1 t. rum extract
1 c. chopped pecans

Stir all ingredients together.

Keep hot appetizers toasty in a 250-degree oven
until serving time.

Warm Brie Spread with Topping

Serves 8

8-oz. round Brie cheese
2 T. sweetened dried cranberries
1 t. fresh thyme, chopped

1 T. chopped walnuts, toasted
assorted crackers

Using a serrated knife, remove top rind from cheese; discard rind. Place cheese in an ungreased one-quart casserole dish, cut-side up. Sprinkle with cranberries and thyme; top evenly with walnuts. Bake, uncovered, at 350 degrees for 15 minutes, or until cheese is soft and warm. Serve immediately with crackers.

The secret to being a relaxed hostess...choose foods
that can be prepared in advance. At party time, simply pull
from the fridge and serve, or pop into a hot oven as needed.

Cranberry Roll-Ups

Makes 3 to 4 dozen

8-oz. container whipped cream
    cheese, softened
8-oz. pkg. crumbled feta cheese
4 green onions, thinly sliced

6-oz. pkg. sweetened dried
    cranberries, chopped
Optional: 2 T. chopped pecans
4 10-inch flour tortillas

In a large bowl, combine all ingredients except tortillas; mix well. Spread mixture evenly on tortillas; roll up. Wrap each in plastic wrap; refrigerate overnight. At serving time, slice each roll into one-inch pieces; arrange on a serving platter.

Section a big stack of chicken wings in a jiffy with sturdy kitchen shears. Afterwards, be sure to wash the shears with plenty of soapy water.

Cranberry Chicken Wings

Makes 12 servings

1 c. fresh cranberries
1 apple, peeled, cored and chopped
zest and juice of 1 orange
1/2 c. water
1/4 c. honey
1 T. soy sauce
1 t. garlic, minced
1 t. cinnamon

1 t. pepper
1/4 c. cornstarch
1 t. chili powder
1/2 t. chipotle powder
1 t. sea salt
4 lbs. chicken wings,
    cut into sections

In a saucepan, combine cranberries, apple, orange zest and juice, water, honey, soy sauce, garlic, cinnamon and pepper. Bring to a boil over medium heat; simmer for about 10 minutes, or until fruit is soft. In a large bowl, mix together cornstarch, spice powders and salt. Add chicken wings; toss to coat. Place wings in a large slow cooker. Spoon fruit sauce mixture over wings; toss to coat. Cover and cook on high setting for about 4 hours, until chicken juices run clear when pierced. Remove wings to a baking sheet. Bake, uncovered, at 400 degrees for about 10 minutes, until sauce is caramelized and golden.

Keep bags of sweetened dried cranberries and chopped walnuts tucked in the cupboard for healthy between-meal snacking.

Cranberry-Dark Chocolate Trail Mix

Makes about 7 cups

10-oz. pkg. dark chocolate chips
   or chunks
6-oz. pkg. sweetened dried
   cranberries

5-oz. pkg. sliced almonds
1 c. walnuts, coarsely chopped
1 c. raisins
Optional: 1/2 c. pistachios

Toss together all ingredients in a large bowl. Store in an airtight container.

Fun-filled snacks for kids big or little.
Fill waffle cones with sliced fresh fruit, then
drizzle fruit with puréed strawberries. Yum!

Dried Fruit & Cream Cheese Roulade   *Serves 15 to 18*

8-oz. pkg. cream cheese, softened
1 T. apricot or apple jelly
1 to 1-1/2 t. water
1/4 c. sweetened dried cranberries, chopped
1/4 c. dried apricots, chopped

1/4 c. chopped dates
1/2 c. crumbled feta cheese or mild goat cheese
1/3 c. chopped pecans or almonds
1 T. fresh chives, chopped
assorted crackers

Place cream cheese between 2 sheets of plastic wrap. With a rolling pin, roll into a 10-inch by 7-inch rectangle. Remove top sheet of plastic wrap; set aside. In a small bowl, mix jelly and enough water make it spreadable. Carefully spread jelly over cheese. Sprinkle with fruits to within 1/2 inch of edges; sprinkle with crumbled cheese. Starting on one long edge, carefully roll up cheese mixture into a log, lifting with the bottom sheet of plastic wrap. Carefully press nuts onto outside of log, rolling slightly to cover all sides. Wrap tightly in plastic wrap. Refrigerate at least 2 to 3 hours, until set. To serve, unwrap log and place on a serving plate; sprinkle with chives. Serve with assorted crackers.

Flea markets offer an amazing variety of table serving pieces for entertaining! Look for vintage china, casseroles and jelly-jar glasses to add old-fashioned charm to your dinner table.

Cranberry-Pineapple Dip

Makes 8 servings

1-1/2 c. shredded Swiss cheese
8-oz. pkg. cream cheese, softened
2/3 c. sweetened dried cranberries

8-oz. can crushed pineapple,
  partially drained
1/2 c. sliced almonds

Combine all ingredients except almonds in an ungreased 2-quart casserole dish. Mix well; sprinkle almonds on top. Bake, uncovered, at 350 degrees for 20 to 25 minutes. Serve warm.

Don't toss out that dab of leftover cranberry sauce!
Purée it with balsamic vinaigrette to create a
tangy salad dressing.

Favorite Festive Cranberry Sauce *Makes about 2 quarts*

2 12-oz. pkgs. fresh cranberries
2-1/4 c. sugar
1 c. water

zest of 2 large oranges
juice of 1 large orange

In a large saucepan over medium-high heat, combine all ingredients. Bring to a boil. Reduce heat to medium; cook until berries are soft and mixture starts to thicken. Let cool slightly; pour into a gelatin mold or into canning jars. Cover and chill.

Festive ice cubes! Drop a couple of cranberries and
a sprig of mint into each section of an ice cube tray. Fill
with distilled water for crystal-clear cubes and freeze.

Jalapeño Cranberry Relish

Serves 8 to 10

1 to 2 jalapeño peppers, halved
  and deveined
12-oz. pkg. fresh cranberries
1 whole orange, quartered

11-oz. can crushed pineapple,
  well drained
1 c. sugar

Remove seeds from jalapeños, if a milder taste is preferred. In a food grinder, grind jalapeños, cranberries and orange. Stir in pineapple and sugar; transfer to a serving bowl. Cover and refrigerate overnight before serving.

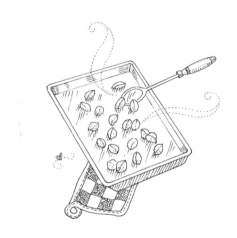

Toasting adds so much flavor to nuts. Spread nuts in
a shallow pan in a single layer. Bake at 350 degrees
for 4 to 6 minutes, until toasted, stirring halfway through.

Aunt Minnie's Marmalade Pork Chops

Makes 6 servings

1 c. pure maple syrup
1 c. brown sugar, packed
2-1/2 c. apple cider or juice
1 c. raisins
1 c. sweetened dried cranberries
1 c. orange or citrus marmalade
6 country-style pork chops,
  thick-cut
2 t. granulated garlic

In a saucepan over medium heat, stir together maple syrup and brown sugar; bring to a low boil. Stir in apple juice, raisins and cranberries; simmer until fruit is soft. Stir in marmalade; cook until simmering. Meanwhile, sprinkle pork chops with garlic; arrange in a lightly greased 13"x9" glass baking pan in a single layer. Spoon half of marmalade mixture over pork chops. Bake, uncovered, at 325 degrees for 30 minutes. Remove from oven; spoon rest of marmalade mixture over pork chops, reserving 1/2 cup in a small bowl. Bake an additional 10 to 15 minutes, until pork chops are done. Serve pork chops with reserved warm marmalade mixture on the side.

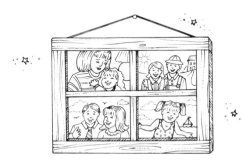

What is a family, after all, except memories?
Haphazard and precious as the contents of
a catch-all drawer in the kitchen.

– Joyce Carol Oates

Harvest Turkey Pot Pie

Makes 6 servings

1/4 c. onion, chopped
1 T. butter
2 10-3/4 oz. cans cream of
    chicken soup
3 c. cooked turkey, cubed
2 McIntosh apples, peeled,
    cored and cubed

1/2 c. fresh cranberries
1 t. lemon juice
1/4 t. cinnamon
1/8 t. poultry seasoning
10-inch pie crust

In a large saucepan over medium heat, sauté onion in butter until tender. Stir in remaining ingredients except pie crust; simmer gently. Spoon turkey mixture into an ungreased 11"x7" baking pan. Roll out pie crust to a 12-inch by 8-inch rectangle. Place over filling in baking pan. Flute edges; cut several slits to vent. Bake at 425 degrees for 15 minutes. Reduce heat to 375 degrees; continue baking for about 35 minutes more, until crust is golden and filling is bubbly. Serve piping hot.

Having steamed veggies on the side? Serve them up
in individual ramekins or, if serving fresh veggies,
use paper muffin cups for a special touch.

Chicken & Cranberry Pasta

Makes 4 to 6 servings

12-oz. pkg. bowtie pasta,
   uncooked
1 c. sweetened dried cranberries
1/3 c. cranberry juice cocktail
1/2 c. green onions, chopped
2 T. butter
1/2 c. all-purpose flour

1 t. paprika
1 t. dried thyme
1/2 t. salt
pepper to taste
1-1/2 lbs. boneless, skinless
   chicken breasts, thinly sliced
16-oz. can chicken broth

Cook pasta according to package directions; drain. Meanwhile, combine cranberries and juice in a microwave-safe bowl; microwave on high setting for one minute and set aside. In a skillet over medium heat, sauté onions in butter for 5 minutes; set aside. Mix flour and seasonings in a plastic zipping bag; add chicken, shaking to coat. Sauté chicken in skillet for 5 minutes; add onions and chicken broth. Simmer 5 to 6 minutes. Drain cranberries; stir into chicken mixture, heating through. Fold in pasta; toss gently.

Make dinners fun for the kids too with a clever table runner
for the kids' table. Sew a border of bandanna print fabric all
around the runner edges. Remove the back pockets from old
jeans and stitch them on each end. Fill pockets with
forks, straws and napkins!

Cranberry Pot Roast

Serves 4 to 6

2 to 3-lb. pork roast or beef
   chuck roast
1/2 c. sugar
salt and pepper to taste

1 T. butter
1/2 c. sherry vinegar
12-oz. pkg. fresh cranberries
juice and zest of one orange

Dredge roast in sugar; reserve any remaining sugar. Sprinkle with salt and pepper; set aside. Melt butter in a deep skillet over medium-high heat. Add roast and brown on all sides. Add vinegar; cook for one minute. Stir in cranberries and reserved sugar; mix in orange juice and zest. Reduce heat to low; cover and simmer for about 2 hours, stirring every 30 minutes.

Candied cranberries are a lovely garnish for roast chicken. In a saucepan, bring one cup water and one cup sugar almost to a boil, stirring until sugar dissolves. Pour into a bowl and add one cup fresh cranberries. Chill overnight; drain well. Toss cranberries with superfine sugar to coat and dry on wax paper.

Chicken Cranberry Ruby

1/3 c. all-purpose flour
1 t. salt
2 lbs. chicken pieces
1/4 c. butter
1-1/2 c. fresh cranberries
3/4 c. sugar

1/4 c. onion, chopped
1 t. orange zest
3/4 c. orange juice
1/4 t. cinnamon
1/4 t. ground ginger

Combine flour and salt in a large plastic zipping bag. Working in batches, add chicken pieces to bag and shake to coat well. Melt butter in a large skillet over medium heat. Cook chicken until golden on all sides, turning once, about 10 minutes. Meanwhile, combine remaining ingredients in a saucepan over medium-high heat; bring to a boil. Pour cranberry mixture over chicken in skillet. Reduce heat to low; cover and cook for 35 to 40 minutes, until chicken is no longer pink in the center and sauce has thickened.

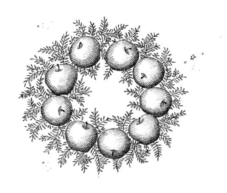

Deck the front door with a little unexpected color...
secure bright green Granny Smith apples with
wire to a traditional greenery wreath.

Honeyed Cranberry Pork Roast

Makes 8 servings

3 to 4-lb. pork roast
salt and pepper to taste
1-1/2 c. fresh cranberries,
   finely chopped

1/2 c. honey
2 t. orange zest
1/4 t. ground cloves
1/2 t. nutmeg

Season roast on all sides with salt and pepper; place in a slow cooker.
Combine remaining ingredients in a bowl; spoon over roast. Cover and
cook on low setting for 8 to 10 hours, until roast is tender and no longer
pink inside.

Enjoy a taste of summer in fall...make an extra favorite
veggie casserole to tuck in the freezer. Wrap well
with plastic wrap and freeze. Thaw overnight in
the refrigerator and bake as usual.

Easy Thanksgiving Dinner

1 T. oil
2-lb. boneless, skinless
  turkey breast
12-oz. pkg. favorite-flavor
  stuffing mix
1 sweet potato, peeled and cubed

1/2 c. celery, chopped
1/2 c. onion, chopped
1/2 c. carrot, peeled and chopped
2 c. chicken broth
1/2 c. chopped walnuts
1/2 c. fresh cranberries

Heat oil in a skillet over medium heat. Sauté turkey in oil until browned on both sides, about 5 minutes; drain. In a slow cooker, combine turkey and remaining ingredients except nuts and cranberries. Cover and cook on low setting for 7 to 8 hours, until turkey is no longer pink in the center. About one hour before serving, stir in walnuts and cranberries.

Instead of serving traditional biscuits or dinner rolls with this dish, bake up some sweet and tangy cranberry muffins! Just stir frozen cranberries into cornbread muffin mix and bake as usual.

Cranberry Cider Chicken

Serves 4 to 6

4 to 6 boneless, skinless chicken
   breasts
2 c. Cranberry Cider
1 T. whole cloves
4 4-inch cinnamon sticks

1 c. sweetened dried cranberries
2 apples, peeled, cored and
   quartered
1 orange, peeled and sectioned
Optional: orange slices

Arrange chicken in a lightly greased roasting pan; pour cider over all.
Place cloves and cinnamon sticks in a square of cheesecloth; tie closed
with kitchen string. Add to roasting pan with cranberries. Bake,
uncovered, at 350 degrees for 2 hours, or until juices run clear when
chicken is pierced. Add apples and orange to roasting pan; return to oven
until orange is warm, about 5 minutes. Garnish servings with slices of
orange, if desired.

Cranberry Cider:

1.2-oz. pkg. mulling spice mix   4 c. cranberry juice cocktail

Combine spice mix and juice in a medium saucepan; bring to steaming
over medium heat. Stir well. Makes 4 cups.

If your slow cooker doesn't have a built-in timer,
pick up an automatic timer at the hardware store and
plug the crock right into it. It's also fine to fill a
slow cooker with chilled ingredients, then set the crock's
timer to start one to 2 hours later.

Grandma's Cranberry Sauce

Makes about 8 pints

2 oranges, chopped
2 oranges, peeled and chopped
4 apples, cored and chopped

2 lbs. fresh cranberries
1 c. sugar

Combine all ingredients in a large slow cooker; stir gently. Cover and cook on low setting for 8 to 9 hours, stirring occasionally, until syrupy and berries have burst. Spoon into freezer containers or sterilized jars. Cover and refrigerate for up to 3 weeks, or freeze for up to 3 months.

For a tasty garnish on salads, use a vegetable peeler to make cheese curls in a jiffy.

Turkey Supper Cranberry Salad

Makes 16 servings

12-oz. pkg. fresh cranberries
2 c. sugar
3 c. water
6-oz. pkg. cherry gelatin mix

2 c. celery, chopped
2 c. apples, peeled, cored
   and diced
1 c. chopped pecans or walnuts

In a large saucepan over medium-high heat, combine cranberries, sugar and water. Bring to a boil; cook and stir for 5 minutes, or until berries are soft. Add dry gelatin mix and stir well. Remove from heat; allow to cool completely. Stir in celery, apples and nuts; transfer to a serving bowl. Cover and chill until set.

Tin cans with colorful, vintage-looking labels make the best country-style vases. Fill several with small bouquets of mums and march them along a windowsill or mantel.

Marie's Ribbon Salad

Serves 10 to 12

3-oz. pkg. lime gelatin mix
3 c. boiling water, divided
1/3 c. unsweetened pineapple juice
1 c. crushed pineapple, drained
1 t. unflavored gelatin
2 T. cold water
8-oz. pkg. cream cheese, softened

1/3 c. milk
2 3-oz. pkgs. strawberry or
  raspberry gelatin mix
14-oz. can whole-berry cranberry
  sauce
Garnish: mayonnaise-style salad
  dressing

Green layer: in a small bowl, dissolve lime gelatin mix in one cup boiling water. Stir in pineapple juice and pineapple. Pour into an 11"x7" glass baking pan; refrigerate until set. White layer: in a small saucepan, sprinkle unflavored gelatin over cold water; let stand for one minute. Cook and stir over low heat until completely dissolved; transfer to a large bowl. Beat in cream cheese and milk until smooth. Spread cream cheese mixture over chilled, set lime layer; refrigerate until set. Red layer: in a small bowl, dissolve strawberry gelatin mix in remaining 2 cups boiling water; stir in cranberry sauce. Cool for 10 minutes. Carefully spoon over chilled, set cream cheese layer. Refrigerate until set. To serve, cut into squares; garnish with a dollop of salad dressing.

If you love fresh cranberries, stock up when they're available and pop unopened bags in the freezer. They'll stay fresh and flavorful for months to come.

Sugar-Free Cranberry Salad

Serves 10

2 whole oranges
1 T. orange zest
12-oz. pkg. fresh cranberries
1 red apple, cored and sliced
11-oz. can crushed pineapple
12 envs. powdered sweetener,
   or to taste

0.6-oz. pkg. sugar-free raspberry
   gelatin mix
2 c. boiling water
Optional: 2/3 c. chopped pecans

Grate one tablespoon orange zest; peel both oranges. Cut each into
8 slices; remove seeds. Place oranges, cranberries and apple into a food
processor. Process until evenly chopped; transfer to a bowl. Add zest,
pineapple with juice and sweetener; set aside. In a separate bowl, dissolve
dry gelatin mix in boiling water. Add to fruit mixture; stir well. Fold in
nuts, if using. Cover and refrigerate until set.

A rustic buffet table...set an old door
on top of hay bales!

Goalpost Apple Slaw

2-1/4 c. red apples, cored
 and cubed
2-1/4 c. green apples, cored
 and cubed
1 c. coleslaw mix
1/3 c. sweetened dried cranberries
1/3 c. chopped walnuts

1 c. sour cream
3 T. lemon juice
1 to 2 T. vinegar
1 T. sugar
1 T. poppy seed
3/4 t. salt
1/8 t. pepper

Lightly toss ingredients in a large bowl until well mixed. Chill for at least one hour before serving.

Stock up on favorite pantry items like vegetables,
pasta and rice when they're on sale. They're so handy
for busy-day meals in a hurry.

Cranberry-Wild Rice Salad

Makes 10 to 12 servings

6-1/2 c. water
1/2 c. chicken broth
2-1/2 c. wild rice, uncooked
1 c. sweetened dried cranberries
1 c. golden raisins
1 c. green onions, chopped
3/4 c. pine nuts, toasted

1/2 c. fresh parsley, chopped
2 T. orange zest
1/2 c. orange juice
1/4 c. cider vinegar
1/2 c. olive oil
salt and pepper to taste

Bring water and broth to a boil in a large saucepan over high heat. Add rice; reduce heat to medium. Cover and simmer until rice is cooked yet slightly firm, about 40 minutes, stirring occasionally. Drain; transfer rice to a large bowl to cool. Add cranberries, raisins, onions, pine nuts, parsley and orange zest; toss to mix and set aside. In a small bowl, whisk together orange juice and vinegar. Slowly whisk in oil. Drizzle dressing over rice; toss to coat. Season with salt and pepper. Cover and refrigerate for 2 to 3 hours. Bring to room temperature before serving.

Spoon servings of salad into individual leaves of
radicchio lettuce. The cup-shaped red leaves
can serve as both a salad bowl and a garnish.

Mixed Greens & Cranberry Salad

Serves 4 to 6

4 c. mixed salad greens
1 Granny Smith apple, cored
   and cubed

1/4 c. crumbled blue cheese
1/4 c. sweetened dried cranberries
1/4 c. toasted chopped pecans

Make Vinaigrette Dressing; set aside. Mix all of the ingredients together in a large salad bowl. Drizzle dressing over salad; toss to mix.

Vinaigrette Dressing:

1/2 t. Dijon mustard
3 T. champagne vinegar

1 t. sugar
1/2 c. light olive oil

Whisk mustard, vinegar and sugar together while slowly adding olive oil until mixture is well blended.

A delicious drizzle for steamed veggies!
Boil 1/2 cup balsamic vinegar, stirring often, until
thickened. So simple and scrumptious.

Crunchy Green Bean Salad

Serves 12

1/2 c. honey
1/8 t. cayenne pepper
1-1/2 c. pecan halves
3 T. sherry vinegar
2 t. Dijon mustard
3/4 t. salt

1/2 c. walnut oil
2 lbs. green beans, trimmed
3/4 c. sweetened dried cranberries
2 heads Belgian endive, trimmed
    and sliced lengthwise
pepper to taste

Stir together honey and cayenne pepper in a saucepan over medium heat until warm. Stir in pecans; pour mixture onto a parchment paper- lined 13"x9" baking pan. Bake, uncovered, at 350 degrees until golden, about 8 to 10 minutes, stirring occasionally. Remove from oven; set aside. Whisk together vinegar, mustard and salt. Slowly drizzle in oil, whisking constantly to blend. Fill a large bowl with ice and water; set aside. Add beans to a stockpot; cover with water and bring to a boil. Cook over medium heat until tender, about 2 minutes. Drain; plunge into ice water. Drain again; pat dry and place beans in a large serving bowl. Toss with vinegar mixture to coat. Add nut mixture and remaining ingredients; toss gently. Serve immediately.

Candy cane-style napkin rings that are
so simple, the kids can make them! Just twist
together red and white pipe cleaners
and slip napkins inside.

Cranberry-Pear Relish

Makes 3 cups

1-1/2 c. sugar
1 c. water
1/4 c. lemon juice
4 to 5 ripe pears, peeled, cored
    and chopped

12-oz. pkg. fresh cranberries
1-1/2 t. lemon zest
1/4 t. cinnamon
1/4 t. allspice

In a saucepan over medium heat, combine water, lemon juice and sugar.
Bring to a boil; simmer for 5 minutes, stirring until sugar dissolves. Add
pears; return to a boil and simmer another 5 minutes. Add cranberries; boil
for 7 minutes, or until berries pop. Remove from heat. Stir in lemon zest
and spices; allow to cool. Spoon into a container; cover and keep
refrigerated up to one week.

Need extra oven space? Try roasting veggies in
the slow cooker. You won't even need to add any water
or oil! The vegetables have enough of their
own water to cook properly.

Fruity Roasted Sweet Potatoes

Serves 4 to 6

3 sweet potatoes, peeled and
    cubed
2 Granny Smith apples, cored,
    peeled and cubed
2 T. olive oil
1 c. fresh cranberries
1 T. honey

1-1/2 T. brown sugar, packed
1-1/2 T. chopped walnuts
1/4 c. sweetened flaked coconut
1 t. ground ginger
1 t. cinnamon
1/4 t. salt

Combine potatoes, apples and oil in a lightly greased 13"x9" baking pan.
Mix well. Sprinkle cranberries over potato mixture and drizzle with honey.
Bake at 450 degrees for 10 minutes. Reduce temperature to 350 degrees;
bake for an additional 45 to 50 minutes, until potatoes are tender.
Meanwhile, mix together remaining ingredients; sprinkle over potato
mixture in pan. Return to oven; bake for an additional 5 minutes.

Fill a bushel basket with a jar of Cinnamon-Cranberry
Applesauce and some fresh-baked scones...give to
a friend for a yummy treat!

Cinnamon-Cranberry Applesauce

Serves 4 to 5

5 to 6 apples, peeled, cored and
   coarsely chopped
1 T. lemon juice
1/4 c. water

1 t. vanilla extract
1/2 t. cinnamon
1 T. brown sugar, packed
1/4 c. sweetened dried cranberries

Place apples in a 3-1/2 to 4-quart slow cooker. Add remaining ingredients
except cranberries; stir to combine. Cover and cook on low setting for 4 to
6 hours, until apples are fork-tender. Mash apples; stir in cranberries.
Cover and cook on low setting for 15 to 30 minutes longer, until
cranberries are plumped. Serve warm or cold.

Molded gelatin salads were everywhere in the 1950s, and they're still a refreshing make-ahead dish. Vintage copper molds can often be found at flea markets... dress up a kitchen wall with a whimsical display.

Cranberry Fruit Conserve

Makes 4 servings

12-oz. pkg. fresh cranberries
1-3/4 c. sugar
1 c. water
1 Granny Smith apple, peeled,
　cored and chopped

zest and juice of 1 orange
zest and juice of 1 lemon
3/4 c. raisins
3/4 c. chopped walnuts or pecans

In a saucepan, combine cranberries, sugar and water. Cook over low heat for 5 minutes, or until cranberries pop. Add apple, citrus zests and juices; continue cooking for 15 minutes. Remove from heat; stir in raisins and nuts. Cover and refrigerate; serve chilled.

Is the whole family coming for dinner? Copy one of
Grandma's tried & true recipes onto a festive card,
then punch a hole in the corner and tie the card to
a napkin with a length of ribbon...a sweet keepsake.

Fruit-Stuffed Acorn Squash

Serves 2 to 4

1 acorn squash, halved or
  quartered and seeds removed
1 apple, peeled, cored and diced
1/4 c. sweetened dried cranberries

brown sugar, honey or maple
  syrup to taste
2 T. butter, sliced
cinnamon and nutmeg to taste

Place squash pieces cut-side up in an ungreased 9"x9" baking pan. Fill squash evenly with fruit; top with desired amount of brown sugar, honey or maple syrup. Dot with butter; sprinkle with spices. Bake, uncovered, at 350 degrees for about 45 minutes, or until tender.

Toss some candied nuts over a salad or side dish for a special touch. To make, whisk one egg white with one teaspoon cold water and toss a pound of shelled nuts in this mixture. Mix one cup sugar, one teaspoon cinnamon and 1/2 teaspoon salt; coat the nuts well. Spread nuts on a greased baking sheet. Bake at 225 degrees for one hour, stirring once or twice. Store in an airtight container.

Merry Sweet Potatoes

6 sweet potatoes
3 T. butter, melted
2 T. orange juice
1/2 t. vanilla extract
1 t. cinnamon

1/2 t. nutmeg
salt and pepper to taste
3/4 c. sweetened dried cranberries
1/2 c. brown sugar, packed
1/2 c. chopped pecans

Wrap sweet potatoes individually in aluminum foil; place on a baking sheet. Bake at 350 degrees for one hour. Allow to cool. Cut each sweet potato in half; scoop out the insides into a large bowl. Discard skins. Add butter, orange juice, vanilla and seasonings; stir until smooth. Fold in cranberries. Pour into an 8"x8" baking pan coated with non-stick vegetable spray. Smooth top with a spoon. Sprinkle brown sugar and pecans over top. Bake, uncovered, at 350 degrees for 15 minutes, or until warmed through.

Be sure to have some take-out containers and
labels on hand to send everyone home with leftovers...
if there are any!

Cranberry Wild Rice

1-1/2 c. wild rice, uncooked
2 14-oz. cans vegetable broth
4-1/2 oz. jar sliced mushrooms
4 green onions, sliced
1 T. butter, melted

1/2 t. salt
1/4 t. pepper
1/2 c. slivered almonds, toasted
1/3 c. sweetened dried cranberries

In a 2 to 3-1/2 quart slow cooker, mix together all ingredients except nuts and berries. Cover and cook on low setting for 4 to 5 hours, until wild rice is tender. Stir almonds and berries into rice mixture. Cover and cook on low setting an additional 15 minutes before serving.

Out of dry bread crumbs for a recipe?
Substitute crushed stuffing mix instead
and it will be just as tasty.

Nutty Sausage & Cranberry Stuffing   *Serves 8 to 10*

16-oz. pkg. cornbread stuffing mix
2 c. chicken broth
1 egg, beaten
1/2 c. butter, divided
1 c. onion, chopped

1 c. celery, chopped
1 c. ground Italian pork sausage,
    browned and drained
1 c. sweetened dried cranberries
1/2 c. chopped pecans

Prepare stuffing mix according to package directions, using broth, egg and
1/4 cup butter; set aside. Sauté onion and celery in remaining butter until
translucent. Stir onion mixture and remaining ingredients into stuffing;
toss well to coat. Spread in a lightly greased 13"x9" baking pan. Cover and
bake at 350 degrees for 30 minutes.

Candied red and green cherries, cut in half, make a pretty
and quick garnish for a holiday Bundt® cake.

Cranberry Caramel Cake

Makes 16 servings

18-1/4 oz. pkg. yellow cake mix
   with pudding
4 eggs, beaten
1 c. eggnog
1/3 c. oil

2 t. pumpkin pie spice
1-1/2 c. fresh or frozen
   cranberries, chopped
1 c. chopped walnuts

In a large bowl, combine dry cake mix, eggs, eggnog, oil and spice. Beat with an electric mixer on low speed for 30 seconds; beat for 2 minutes on medium speed. Fold in cranberries and walnuts. Pour batter into a greased and lightly floured 12-cup fluted tube pan. Bake at 350 degrees for 45 to 55 minutes, until a toothpick inserted near center comes out clean. Cool in pan for 10 minutes. Invert cake onto a wire rack; remove pan and cool for about one hour. Drizzle warm Caramel Sauce over cake before serving.

Caramel Sauce:

1/2 c. butter
1-1/4 c. brown sugar, packed

2 T. light corn syrup
1/2 c. whipping cream

Melt butter in a saucepan over medium-high heat. Stir in brown sugar and corn syrup; bring to a boil. Cook for one minute or until sugar dissolves, stirring constantly. Stir in cream. Return to a boil, stirring constantly. Remove from heat.

The crackle of a warm, cozy fire brings everyone together.
Enjoy a simple dinner of roasted hot dogs or toasty pie-iron
sandwiches and mugs of warm spiced cider in front of the
fireplace. A pan of Baked Stuffed Apples in the oven for
dessert will fill the house with a delicious scent.

Baked Stuffed Apples

Makes 4 servings

4 Granny Smith apples
1/3 c. sweetened dried cranberries
1/3 c. chopped walnuts
1/3 c. brown sugar, packed
1-1/2 t. pumpkin pie spice

1/4 c. pure maple syrup
1 T. butter, melted
1/2 c. apple juice
Optional: vanilla ice cream

With an apple corer, scoop out the core and seeds of each apple from the top. Make the opening fairly wide; do not cut through to the bottom. Set aside. In a bowl, mix together cranberries, walnuts, brown sugar and spice. Stuff apples full of cranberry mixture; arrange in a 9"x9" glass baking pan. Combine maple syrup and butter in a cup; drizzle over apples. Pour apple juice around apples. Cover with aluminum foil; bake at 350 degrees for 40 minutes. Uncover; bake for about 20 minutes longer, until bubbly and very tender. Serve warm, garnished with a scoop of ice cream, if desired.

When baking two sheets of cookies at once, remember to reverse the top and bottom sheets halfway through the baking time to ensure they bake evenly.

Judy's Brownie Cookies

Makes 2 dozen

20-oz. pkg. brownie mix
1-1/2 c. quick-cooking oats,
   uncooked
1/2 c. oil

2 eggs, beaten
1/2 c. semi-sweet chocolate chips
1/2 c. sweetened dried cranberries
Optional: pecan halves

In a large bowl, combine dry brownie mix, oats, oil and eggs; mix well.
Stir in chocolate chips and cranberries. Drop dough by rounded teaspoons
onto ungreased baking sheets. If desired, press 3 to 4 pecan halves onto
the top of each cookie. Bake, one sheet at a time, at 350 degrees for
15 to 17 minutes. Let cookies cool for 2 minutes; remove to wire racks
and cool completely.

Baking a homemade pie for a friend? Surprise her
by delivering it in a pretty woven pie basket or
a ceramic pie plate to keep. She'll love it...
two gifts in one!

Cranberry-Walnut Cobbler

2-1/2 c. fresh or frozen
   cranberries
3/4 c. chopped walnuts
1/2 c. plus 3/4 c. sugar, divided
2 eggs, beaten

3/4 c. butter, melted and slightly
   cooled
1/4 t. almond extract
1 c. all-purpose flour
1/8 t. salt

In an ungreased 9" pie plate, combine cranberries, walnuts and 1/2 cup sugar. Toss until coated; set aside. In a bowl, whisk together eggs, melted butter, remaining sugar and extract until blended. Fold in flour and salt until combined. Pour batter over cranberry mixture. Bake at 350 degrees for 40 minutes, or until bubbly and crust is golden. Set pie plate on a wire rack to cool.

Baking lots of cookies and only have one or two baking sheets? Simply line each sheet with parchment paper. As each batch of cookies comes out of the oven, lift off the paper (cookies and all) onto a wire rack. Cool the hot baking sheet under running water and pat it dry...ready for you to add the next round of cookies.

Red, White & Blue Cookies

Makes 6 dozen

1/2 c. butter, softened
1/2 c. shortening
1/2 c. sugar
1/2 c. brown sugar, packed
1 egg, beaten
1 t. vanilla extract
1 t. baking soda

1 t. cream of tartar
1/4 t. salt
2 c. all-purpose flour
1 c. white chocolate chips
2/3 c. sweetened dried cranberries
1/3 c. sweetened dried blueberries

In a very large bowl, combine butter, shortening and sugars; beat until light and fluffy. Add egg; mix well. Add vanilla, baking soda, cream of tartar and salt. Beat in flour; mix well. Fold in remaining ingredients. Roll into walnut-size balls. Place on lightly greased baking sheets, about 2 inches apart. Bake at 350 degrees for 8 to 10 minutes, until golden and firm to the touch. Cool cookies on baking sheets for 2 minutes, until set. Remove to wire racks to cool completely.

A pizza cutter is handy for cutting brownies and
bar cookies neatly. Dip the cutter into
warm water between cuts.

Fruity Popcorn Bars

Makes 16 bars

3-oz. pkg. microwave popcorn, popped
3/4 c. white chocolate chips
3/4 c. sweetened dried cranberries
1/2 c. sweetened flaked coconut

1/2 c. slivered almonds, coarsely chopped
10-oz. pkg. marshmallows
3 T. butter

Line a 13"x9" baking pan with aluminum foil; spray lightly with non-stick vegetable spray. Toss together popcorn, chocolate chips, cranberries, coconut and almonds in a large bowl; set aside. Melt marshmallows and butter in a saucepan over medium heat; stir until smooth. Pour over popcorn mixture and toss to coat completely; quickly pour into prepared pan. Lay a sheet of wax paper over top and press down firmly. Chill for 30 minutes, or until firm. Lift bars from pan, using foil as handles; peel off foil and wax paper. Slice into bars and chill an additional 30 minutes.

It's easy to make pie crust garnishes! Just use tiny cookie cutters to cut shapes from a homemade or store-bought pie crust. Arrange cut-outs on a baking sheet lined with parchment paper. Lightly spritz with non-stick vegetable spray and sprinkle with cinnamon. Bake at 350 degrees for about 6 minutes, or until golden. Cool.

Cranberry-Pecan White Chocolate Pie

Makes 8 servings

1 c. fresh cranberries
1 c. pecan halves
1 c. white chocolate chips
9-inch pie crust, unbaked
3 eggs, beaten

3/4 c. dark brown sugar, packed
3/4 c. light corn syrup
2 T. all-purpose flour
1 t. orange zest

Layer cranberries, pecans and chocolate chips in unbaked pie crust; set aside. In a bowl, stir together remaining ingredients; blend well and pour into crust. Set pie plate on a baking sheet. Bake at 400 degrees for 25 minutes. Remove from oven; cover pie with a piece of aluminum foil coated with non-stick vegetable spray. Bake an additional 10 to 15 minutes, until crust is golden and filling is set in center.

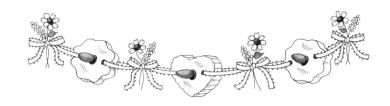

String together some old-fashioned cookie cutters with
a cheery ribbon and add your own embellishments...
what a festive addition to your Christmas kitchen!

Cranberry-Pear Streusel Pie

Serves 6 to 8

1 c. sweetened dried cranberries,
   chopped
1-1/2 c. orange juice
9-inch deep-dish pie crust,
   unbaked

1/3 c. sugar
1/4 c. all-purpose flour
1 t. pumpkin pie spice
3 15-oz. cans sliced pears,
   drained

Combine cranberries and orange juice in a bowl. Refrigerate for several
hours; drain. Bake pie crust at 350 degrees until lightly golden, about
15 minutes; cool. In a large bowl, mix sugar, flour and spice; add pears
and cranberries. Spoon into crust. Spread Streusel Topping evenly over pie.
Bake at 350 degrees until golden, 30 to 40 minutes.

Streusel Topping:

1 c. all-purpose flour
1/2 c. brown sugar, packed

1 t. orange extract
1/2 c. chilled butter

Mix together all ingredients with a fork until crumbly.

INDEX

INDEX

Our Story

Back in 1984, we were next-door neighbors raising our families in the little town of Delaware, Ohio. Two moms with small children, we were looking for a way to do what we loved and stay home with the kids too. We had always shared a love of home cooking and making memories with family & friends and so, after many a conversation over the backyard fence, **Gooseberry Patch** was born.

We put together our first catalog at our kitchen tables, enlisting the help of our loved ones wherever we could. From that very first mailing, we found an immediate connection with many of our customers and it wasn't long before we began receiving letters, photos and recipes from these new friends. In 1992, we put together our very first cookbook, compiled from hundreds of these recipes and, the rest, as they say, is history.

Hard to believe it's been over 35 years since those kitchen-table days! From that original little **Gooseberry Patch** family, we've grown to include an amazing group of creative folks who love cooking, decorating and creating as much as we do. Today, we're best known for our homestyle, family-friendly cookbooks, now recognized as national bestsellers.

One thing's for sure, we couldn't have done it without our friends all across the country. Each year, we're honored to turn thousands of your recipes into our collectible cookbooks. Our hope is that each book captures the stories and heart of all of you who have shared with us. Whether you've been with us since the beginning or are just discovering us, welcome to the **Gooseberry Patch** family!

Visit our website anytime
www.gooseberrypatch.com

Email

JoAnn & Vickie

1·800·854·6673